Princess Diana

A True Fairy Tale

Kay Stammers

This book is written in loving memory of
Diana, Princess of Wales (1961–1997),
to share her story with the children of the world.

First published in Australia in 1997 by
Thomas C. Lothian Pty Ltd
11 Munro Street, Port Melbourne,
Victoria 3207

Photograph credits:
Austral: front cover (Lord Lichfield), 15, 20, 23, 25, 32 (de Marchelier),
back cover (Tim Graham); Press Association of London:
1, 4, 6, 7, 8, 10, 11, 12, 14, 16, 18, 21, 22, 30;
AP/AAP: 3, 19, 26, 27, 28, 29; Profile Press: 5, 9; Reuters: 13, 17,
24, 31, front inside flap: Reuters; back inside flap: David Anderson.
(Page 1 drawing by the late Madame Pawlikowska, 1965.)

Princess Diana
A True Fairy Tale
Text copyright © 1997 by Kay Stammers
Illustrations / design copyright © 1997 by Tristan Parry
Produced by Strawberry Ram, a division of Media One Pty Ltd.
Printed in the U.S.A. All rights reserved.
http://www.harperchildrens.com

Library of Congress catalog card number: 98-70348
ISBN 0-06-107119-6

1   2   3   4   5   6   7   8   9   10
❖
First American edition, 1998

Once upon a time, in the green countryside of England, lived a little girl named Lady Diana. Her father, Lord Spencer, was a rich farmer. They lived in Park House on the royal estate of Sandringham, next door to the holiday home of the Queen. The grand old house was surrounded by gardens and orchards, and forests and fields, which in summer were yellow with ripening corn.

Lady Diana was very pretty, with golden hair
and big blue eyes. She lived with her mother
and father, baby brother and two older
sisters. There was also a cook, a housekeeper, a
governess and a nanny. They used to spoil the
children and give them extra treats when their
parents were not looking.

iana loved to run with her dogs, ride her
pony and look after her baby brother.
Sometimes she would stroll with her mother
and sisters along the leafy country lanes to the nearby
village. When the Queen and her family came up
from London, Diana often went to play with the two
younger princes, Edward and Andrew, who were
about the same age as herself.

One day, when Diana was six, something happened that made her feel very sad. Her mother and father said they had stopped loving each other, and they wanted to get a divorce. Her mother was going to marry another man and live with him far away. The children were going to stay in the family house with their father. Diana had tears in her eyes as she waved good-bye to her mother.

iana missed her mother very much. But she had to be brave for her brother's sake. He was only three, and she often had to comfort him when he cried.

Their father did everything he could to make the children happy. He knew Diana loved animals, so when she turned seven he had a great birthday surprise—a real camel on the grounds of Park House to give rides to all the children.

When she was a bit older, Diana was sent to boarding school. She made lots of new friends. Her favorite subjects were music, dancing and gym. She always won the swimming and diving competitions.

On holidays she often went to stay with her mother and her mother's new husband, Diana's stepfather. They lived on an island off the coast of Scotland, where the children could spend all day boating, fishing and swimming. It was great fun.

iana's grandfather was an earl, and he lived in a huge house called Althorp, which had been in Diana's family for generations. It was set in rolling green fields. When she was thirteen, her grandfather died, and her father became the new earl. This meant they had to leave Park House and go to live at Althorp.

Althorp House was a wonderful place to live. It had a lovely blue lake with a little green island in the middle. Diana and her brother used to row their small boat across to the island and sit on the bank under a willow tree, listening to the sound of the birds.

Around this time, their father decided to get married again. Now Diana had two sets of parents. She didn't much like the idea of having a stepmother—she still wanted her real mother back again. But she loved her father, so she tried to be nice to his new wife.

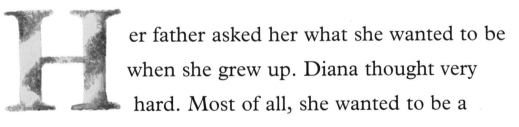

Her father asked her what she wanted to be when she grew up. Diana thought very hard. Most of all, she wanted to be a ballet dancer but, sadly, she was too tall. She also loved babies and enjoyed looking after her little brother, so she thought she might be a kindergarten teacher instead. A few years later when she finished school, that's exactly what she did.

When she was seventeen, Diana moved to the big city of London. Soon she found a job in a kindergarten. The children all loved her, and she looked forward to seeing them each morning. She enjoyed teaching them new things, but most of all she enjoyed making them laugh. Diana felt she was doing something really worthwhile with her life, and she was very happy.

Around that time, the Queen's oldest son, Prince Charles, was looking for a bride. The Queen felt it was time for him to get married, but Charles hadn't yet found the right person.

Prince Charles loved hunting for foxes and pheasants in the forests around Sandringham. After the hunts, they would all go back to the main house for a huge feast.

One autumn, Diana's father held a big hunt and invited the Prince. Diana had never liked hunting or shooting animals, but this weekend she went along to be with her family and friends, and to meet the Prince.

As soon as Prince Charles saw Diana, his heart leaped. When they were children, she used to play with his little brothers in the royal gardens, but he hadn't taken much notice of her then. Now she had become a sweet and charming young woman, with a carefree laugh and sparkling eyes—a woman fit to be a princess.

The Prince plucked up his courage and invited her to come sailing with him on the royal yacht. Diana was rather shy, and her cheeks blushed crimson red as she smiled and said yes.

he Prince and Lady Diana went out together many times, and they fell in love. Soon the newspapers heard of the romance.

One morning when Diana arrived at the kindergarten, she found a group of photographers waiting for her at the gate. The cameras snapped and flashed, and everyone shouted out questions about her and the Prince. Diana didn't know what to say.

The next morning, her picture was on the front page of every newspaper in the country. Somehow she knew that from this day on her life would never be the same.

ne evening, the Prince took Diana to
dinner at the Palace to meet the Queen
and the rest of the Royal Family. Diana was
very shy and rather nervous, but everyone seemed to
like her. After dinner, Prince Charles led her into his
private sitting room. He took a small silver box from
his pocket and gave it to Diana. Inside, resting on
deep-blue velvet, was a sparkling diamond and
sapphire ring.

"Diana, will you marry me?" asked the Prince.

And so they were married. It was a grand wedding, one of the grandest the world had ever seen. Diana was driven to St. Paul's Cathedral in a golden carriage drawn by four white horses. Crowds of people lined the streets calling her name and throwing flowers in her path. It seemed that everyone in the land had come to London to see the new princess.

When Diana stepped out of the carriage, the crowds gasped. She looked just like a fairy princess. She was dressed in a gown of ivory silk trimmed with lace, ribbons and pearls, with a long flowing veil and a sparkling diamond tiara. She held an enormous bunch of white roses and orchids. Her smile was so dazzling, it made all hearts melt.

By the time the clock struck twelve, Lady Diana had become Her Royal Highness, Princess Diana, wife of the Prince of Wales.

oon they had two children—Prince William, and his little brother, Prince Harry.

Princess Diana adored her sons. Along with looking after her new family, Diana had to learn how to do many other important jobs, like making speeches, helping people who were sick and poor and visiting other countries in the kingdom and around the world. Everywhere the Princess went, crowds came to see her. She was so kind and so beautiful that everyone loved her.

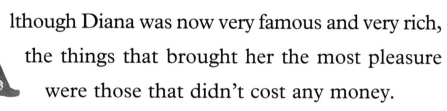

Although Diana was now very famous and very rich, the things that brought her the most pleasure were those that didn't cost any money.

Her two boys were more precious to her than all the gold and jewels in the palace. She loved teaching them about the world. Instead of keeping the young princes inside the palace, she often took them to ordinary places like the streets, the supermarket and the movies, so they could enjoy simple pleasures like other children.

ut Princess Diana's happiness was not to last. Her husband, Prince Charles, told her he was not in love with her anymore, and that they must separate. Diana was brokenhearted. She remembered how sad she had been when her own parents had separated, and she didn't want her little boys to suffer the same sadness. But there was nothing to be done.

Diana stayed in their home at Kensington Palace, and the Prince moved out. By now her two boys were going to boarding school, but she saw them as often as she could, on weekends and during the holidays. They had such fun together. She sent them lots of letters and presents and made sure they knew that she and Prince Charles still loved them very much, even though they were no longer married.

Although Diana was sad, she continued her good work helping others. She visited sick people in the hospital and went to far away lands to comfort poor and starving children. She no longer traveled in fine carriages or had lots of servants to look after her, but the people still loved her.

"Now that I am no longer married to Prince Charles, I will never be Queen of this country," she told them. "But I'd rather do good deeds and be Queen of your hearts."

As time went by, the Princess grew used to being on her own. She thought she would be sad and alone forever. Then one day she met a man named Dodi Fayed. Dodi was dark and handsome, and very rich. Like Diana, he had a kind heart and twinkling eyes, and he loved animals and children.

That summer, Dodi invited the Princess to come for a holiday in France to go swimming and sailing. Her boys came too. They all had a wonderful time together. At last, Diana was truly happy again.

Dodi's father owned the Ritz, one of the finest hotels in Paris. Diana and Dodi had a wonderful dinner together in the dining room. Afterward, Dodi had a surprise for Diana—an exquisite gold and diamond ring. Diana was so happy, she thought her heart would burst.

And that's almost the end of the story, for a terrible, terrible thing happened. That night, when Diana and Dodi were being driven through the streets of Paris, their car crashed. Dodi and the driver were killed. Diana was rushed to the hospital by an ambulance, but the doctors couldn't save her. Princess Diana had died.

The whole world cried. They cried for their beloved Princess, they cried for her handsome Dodi, and they cried for the two boys she had left behind—Prince William, who was now fifteen, and Prince Harry, who was only twelve. Both of them would have to face the future without their darling mother, who had brought them so much love and joy.

The whole world mourned.

During the next week, thousands and thousands of people came to the Palace gates to lay flowers on the footpath in memory of the Princess. The piles of flowers grew higher and higher, and stretched further and further, until it seemed the whole of London was filled with beautiful scents that wafted in the air and mingled with the tears of the people.

n Saturday, September 6, 1997, Princess Diana's funeral was held in one of England's greatest churches, Westminster Abbey. Friends flew in from all over the world. There were many famous people—politicians, film directors, actors and singers—as well as many people who had worked with Diana to help raise money for the sick and poor. The pop star Elton John sang a special song for Diana, called "Candle in the Wind."

After the funeral service, the car carrying Diana's coffin drove slowly through the streets of London, and north through the countryside, to the sleepy village near Althorp, where Diana had grown up. All along the way, people lined the roads and threw flowers in her path, just as they had done when Diana had married all those years ago. Soon the shiny black car was covered with flowers.

rincess Diana was
buried under a
carpet of flowers on the
little green island in the middle of the lake—the same
place she had loved coming
to when she was a child.

Now it will always be her
special place, and her sons,
her brother, and the rest of
her family will be able to
visit her in peace.

 The beautiful Princess Diana will live in our hearts forever. And her soul still shines brightly in her two brave boys— Prince Harry, and Prince William, the boy who will one day be king.